Table of Contents

Style	Page
Classic One Loop	3
Floating Square Knot	4
The Magic Trick	5
Cowboy Scarf Tie	6
The Hidden Knot (or Bunny Ear)	7
The Turtleneck	8
The Butterfly Wrap	9
The Chain Knot	10
The Double Roll	11
The Rolled Ring	12
The Braid	13
The French Twist	14
The Infinity Tie	15
The Waterfall	16
The Simple Bolero	17
The Decoration	18
The Lady's Half Windsor	19
The Ascot	20
The Buckaroo	22
The Kelly Wrap	23

Introduction

Scarves - that little bit of magic that can turn a good look into something spectacular, take a so-so outfit and give it a zing.

Great for all kinds of weather and every season, they are versatile and beautiful. Go frilly or funky, sophisticated or sporty - scarves can go any way you want them to.

Romantic, sexy or cloud-soft and dreamy, their ability to change our mood and our look are almost without limit.

Here is a small beginning to learning to tie them that will get you started on the road to becoming your own scarf sensation.

Have fun! Be daring! Be yourself, and never be afraid to go your own way. Such a simple, easy and elegant way to give yourself a little fashion freedom and style all your own.

Knot 1: The Classic One Loop

Step 1 — Square Scarf folded to a triangle

Step 2 — Throw scarf over your head so triangle point is going down your back.

Step 3 — Wrap the long end around your neck.

Step 4 — Fluff the triangle and pull both ends to lie evenly on either side.

This is a great tie for a scarf with reverse pattern bringing in contrasting colors where one side is darker than the other. Really shows off the contrast nicely.

This also works with a long rectangular scarf. Just 'put it on backwards' so the center of the scarf is across the front of your neck and bring the two ends across the back of the neck and down the front of the shoulders, forming an X in the back of the neck.

This is a great tie for graduated color rectangle scarves where the color goes from dark to light from the center to the ends or vice versa - the two ends will match and provide nice contrast to the center which wraps the neck.

Knot 2: Floating Square Knot

Step 1
Drape the scarf around your neck with one end hanging longer than the other.

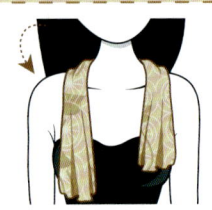

Step 2
Take the longer end, bring it over and up through the shorter end to create the first tie in the knot.

Step 3
Now bring the longer end down and behind the shorter end to create a loop and pass the long end back through the loop you just created and pull.

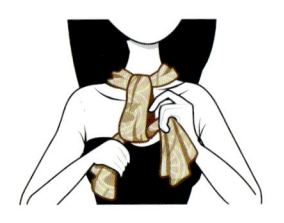

Great tie for a square kerchief folded on the bias or for a longer lightweight oblong scarf folded narrow. This tie creates a square face on a slip knot making it adjustable to wear up close under the neck or loose down the front.

Knot 3: The Magic Trick

Step 1 — Wrap the scarf around the neck completely one time (in the manner of the Classic One Loop.)

Step 2 — Gently loosen the scarf in the front of the One Loop close to the neck and reach down behind it to pull up a section of the scarf hanging in front into a loop that now comes out of the top of the single loop of the scarf.

Step 3 — Now pass the opposite end of the scarf through the loop you have formed with the other end of the scarf.

Step 4 — Rotate the knot and fluff.

This style works best with a long rectangular scarf.

Knot 4: Cowboy Scarf Tie

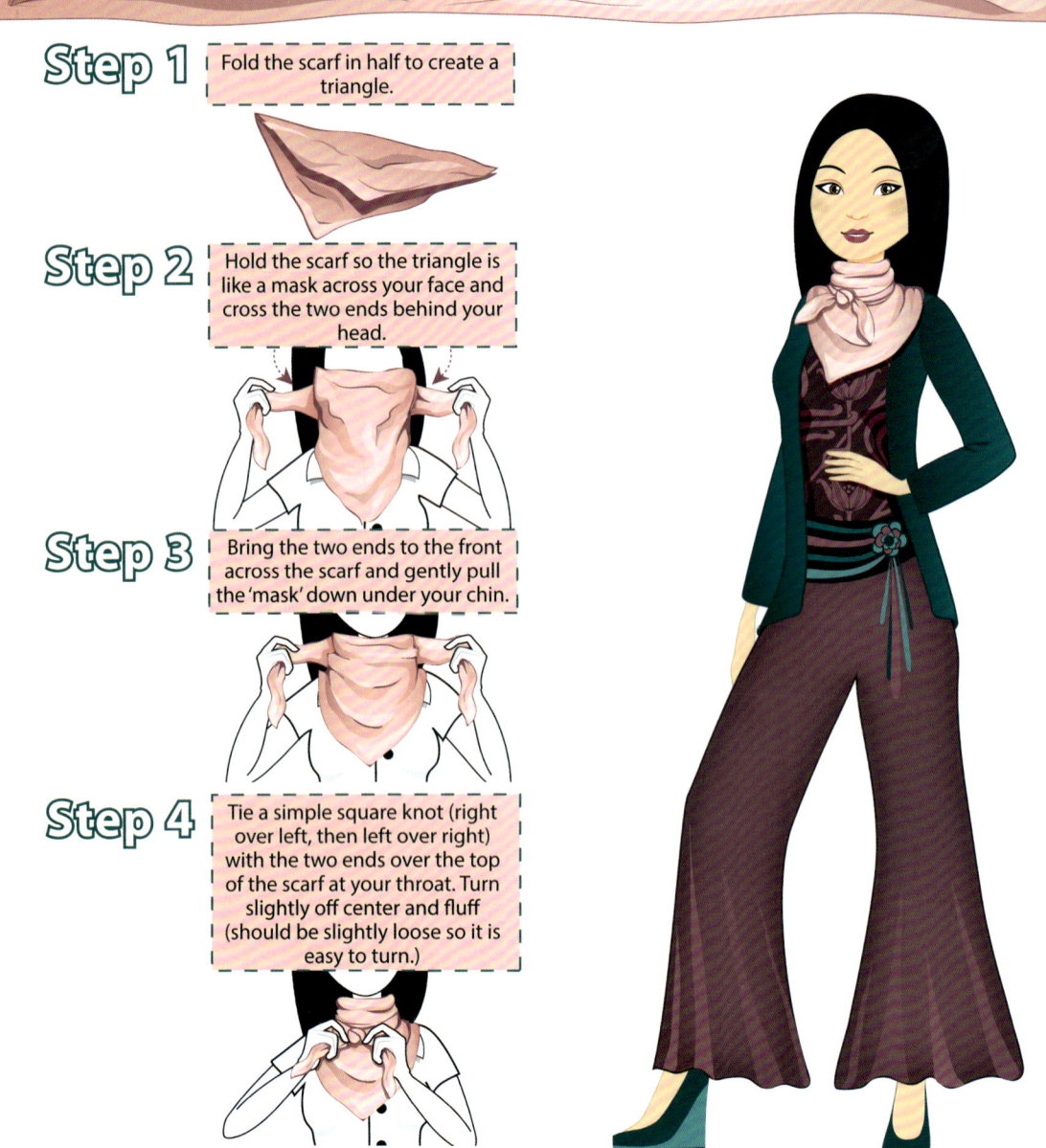

Step 1: Fold the scarf in half to create a triangle.

Step 2: Hold the scarf so the triangle is like a mask across your face and cross the two ends behind your head.

Step 3: Bring the two ends to the front across the scarf and gently pull the 'mask' down under your chin.

Step 4: Tie a simple square knot (right over left, then left over right) with the two ends over the top of the scarf at your throat. Turn slightly off center and fluff (should be slightly loose so it is easy to turn.)

Optional Look: Pull the triangle pieces up from behind the knot so that the knot is underneath the triangle ends. Fluff as needed.

Another way to tie this knot if you have trouble passing the ends behind your head is to drape the scarf over your shoulders with the ends in the front, cross the two ends, and turn the scarf 180 degrees so the two ends come back to the front over the triangle of the scarf and then tie your square knot.

Knot 5: The Hidden Knot (or Bunny Ear)

Step 1 — Square Scarf folded to a triangle

Step 2 — Throw scarf over your shoulders with point down the back. Pull one side of the scarf until the back point is over one shoulder. Continue to pull and wrap so that the back triangle ends up in front.

Step 3 — Wrap once more and bring the end to the front.

Step 4 — Tuck the end from above behind the last wrap and tie in a single tie to the other end of the scarf.

Step 5 — Pull the two ends down and apart, and fluff the wrap over the knot so it is hidden.

This wrap will only produce the bunny ears with a square scarf folded to a triangle for those pointy ears. Done with a rectangular scarf it is called the 'hidden knot' tie.

Knot 6: The Turtleneck

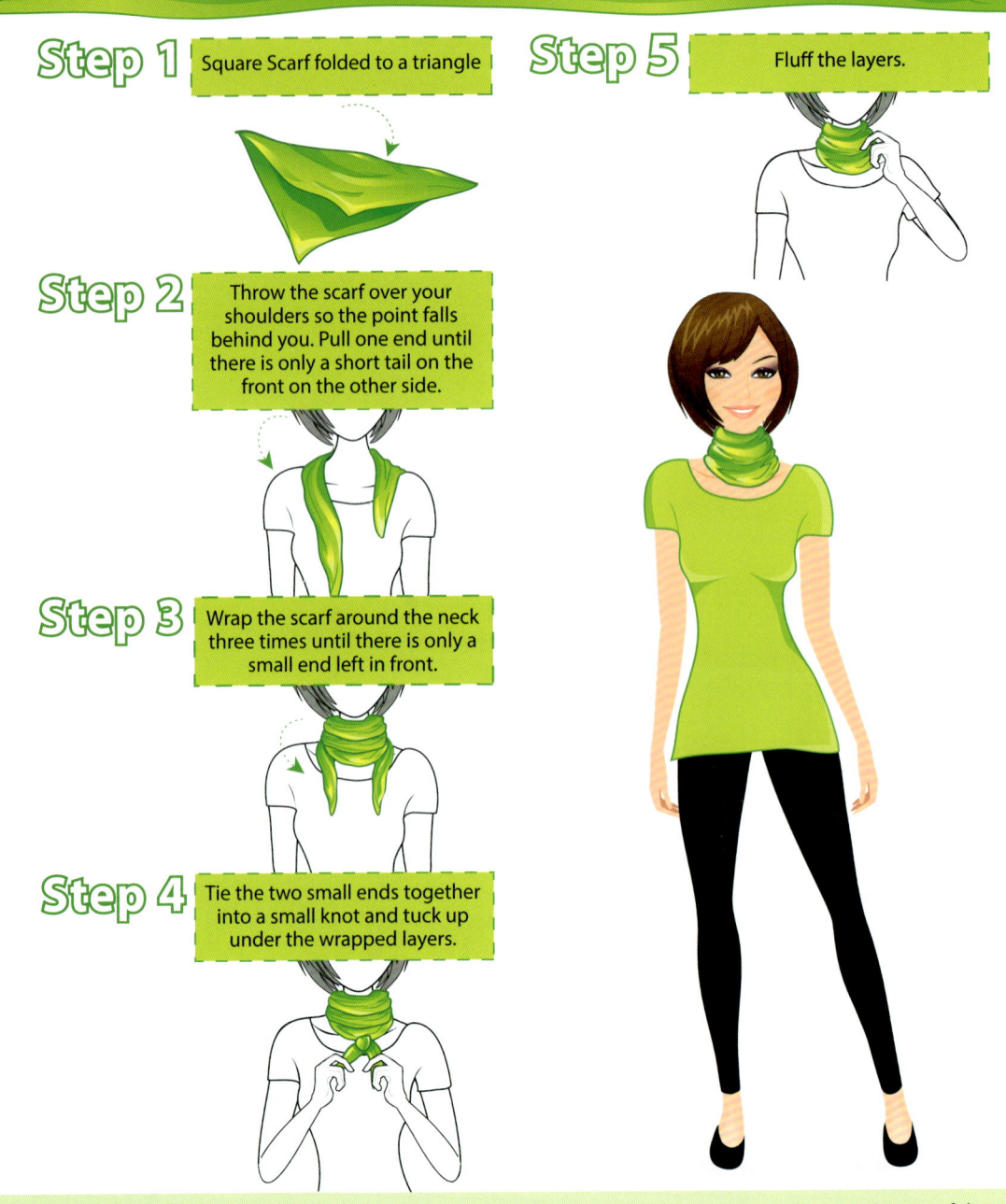

Step 1 — Square Scarf folded to a triangle

Step 2 — Throw the scarf over your shoulders so the point falls behind you. Pull one end until there is only a short tail on the front on the other side.

Step 3 — Wrap the scarf around the neck three times until there is only a small end left in front.

Step 4 — Tie the two small ends together into a small knot and tuck up under the wrapped layers.

Step 5 — Fluff the layers.

This is a great look to go under an open stand-up collared jacket or shirt that lets it peak out at the top of the jacket. It's a great way to wear a highly patterned scarf as an accent to solid color tops.

Knot 7: The Butterfly Wrap

Step 1 — Drape the scarf around your neck so the two ends hang in the front, split about 1/3 to 2/3 lengths.

Step 2 — Take the long end, cross over the short end and come up the back in the center and then down the front to create the first tie.

Step 3 — Take hold of both the ends and pull slightly to tighten.

Step 4 — Hold both ends with one hand and use the other hand to wrap the long end behind the short end of the scarf.

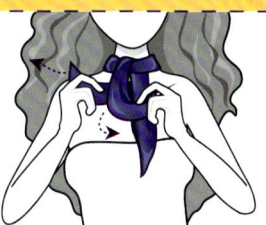

Step 5 — Then create a half bow by pulling a portion of the long end through the loop you just formed. Cinch the knot by pulling on the bow with one hand and the short end with the other.

Use a square scarf folded on the bias or a long scarf with straight lengthwise folds.

Knot 8: Chain Knot

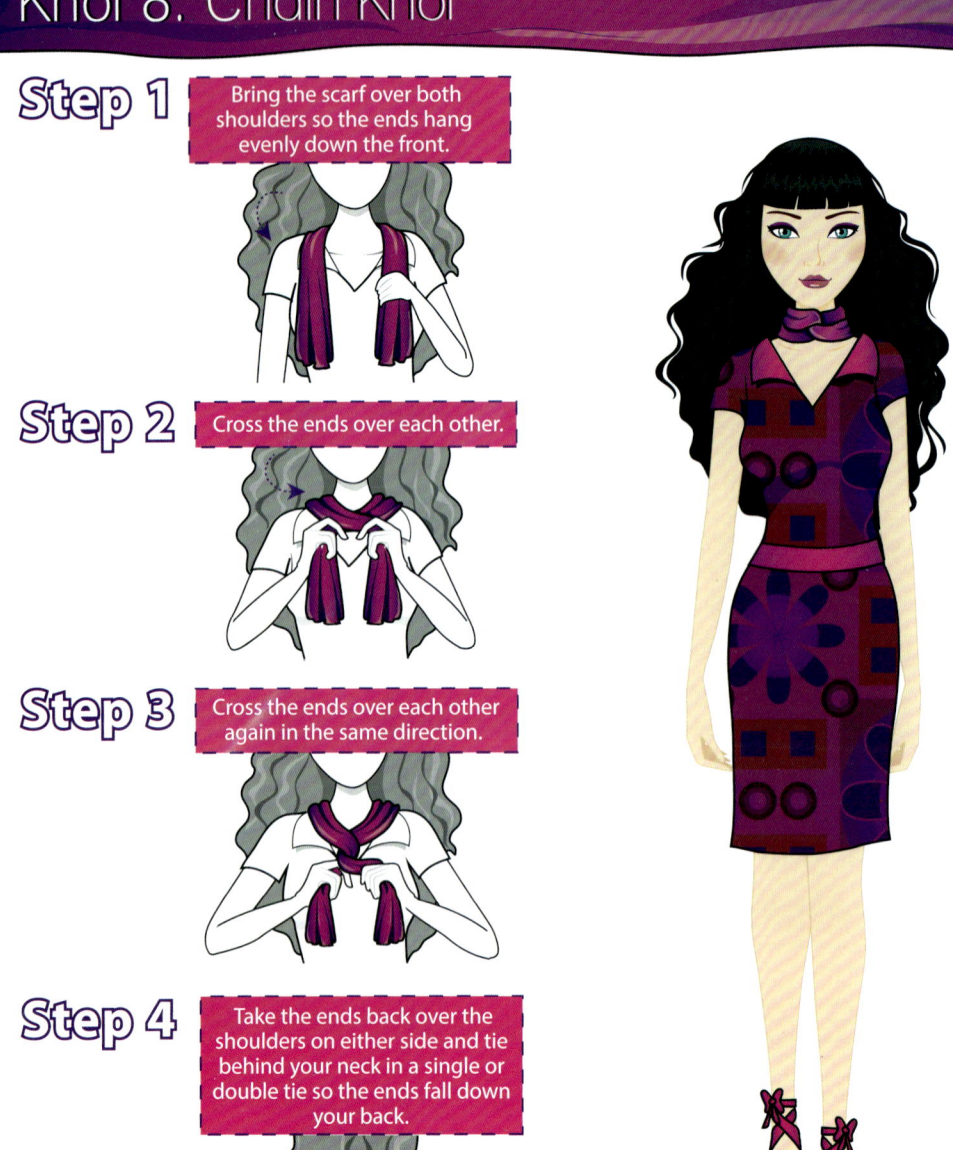

Step 1 — Bring the scarf over both shoulders so the ends hang evenly down the front.

Step 2 — Cross the ends over each other.

Step 3 — Cross the ends over each other again in the same direction.

Step 4 — Take the ends back over the shoulders on either side and tie behind your neck in a single or double tie so the ends fall down your back.

Works best with a long rectangular scarf or a large square scarf folded on the bias.

Knot 9: The Double Roll

Step 1 — Drape the scarf over your shoulders and pull one end until only a short 'tail' is left on your first shoulder (about 8 to 10 inches).

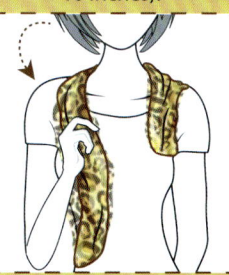

Step 2 — Gently roll the scarf with an inward motion from the top starting at the neck and working out the long end wrapping it around the neck once it is rolled.

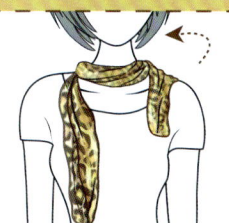

Step 3 — Continue to roll and Wrap it a second time.

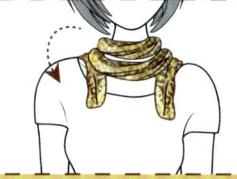

Step 4 — Then tuck in the remaining tail behind the top roll and out between the two rolls.

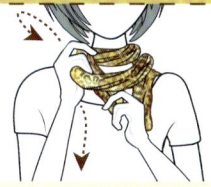

Step 5 — Pull the tail to the back and do the same with the first tail, draping the tails backwards over the shoulder blades.

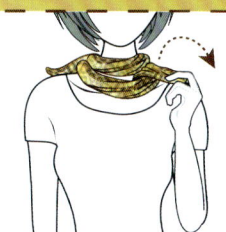

This tie is best with a large lightweight rectangular printed scarf.

Knot 10: The Rolled Ring

Step 1 — Wrap the scarf around the neck one time, holding it so that both the ends are of equal length after the wrap.

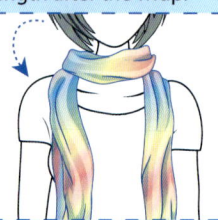

Step 2 — Take the end you just wrapped around and tuck it into the neck of the scarf where a second wrap would start (over the shoulder).

Step 3 — Tuck it in from the top and pull it out so that it wraps the scarf around the neck and repeat this until you get to the back.

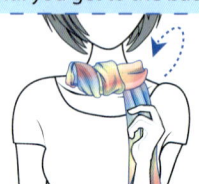

Step 4 — Then take the other end and do the same thing in the opposite direction. You can leave a little 'tail' at the back of the neck.

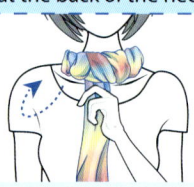

This wrap is good with a long scarf, either a large lightweight cashmere or pashmina work well for this tie.

Knot 11: The Braid

Step 1
Fold the scarf in half and hold the loop where it folds in one hand. Wrap the ends around the neck and push them through the loop in your hand. Pull to snug. That's the European loop.

Step 2
To make the braid, keep hold of the loop and pull it away from the ends already pushed through. Twist the loop and pull the ends through the new loop created by the twisting motion.

Step 3
Adjust and straighten so the braid is centered down the front.

This knot works best with a nice thick winter scarf or a large rectangle scarf.

The Parisian Loop at right is a variation of this tie: Pull the ends separately through the two loops, one end through the first loop and the other end through the second.

13

Knot 12: French Twist

Step 1 — Fold the scarf on the bias into a thin band.

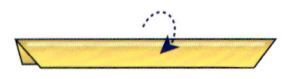

Step 2 — Take the band in both hands and twist until the scarf is twisted almost to the ends. Do not over twist or it will look wrong.

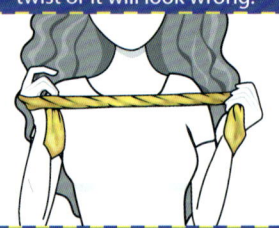

Step 3 — Hold the scarf up in front of your neck, bringing the ends to the back of the neck.

Step 4 — Cross the ends over and bring them back to the front of the neck. Be sure to lay them next to and not on top of the first layer of the scarf.

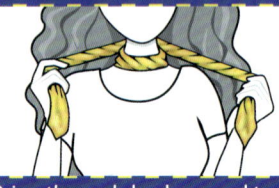

Step 5 — Bring the ends back around to the back and tie them off in a double knot.

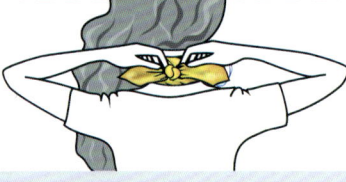

Step 6 — Tuck the loose ends under the twisted scarf at the back. Adjust as necessary to get all three twists to lay flat next to each other.

This style uses a large square silk scarf.

Knot 13: The Infinity Tie

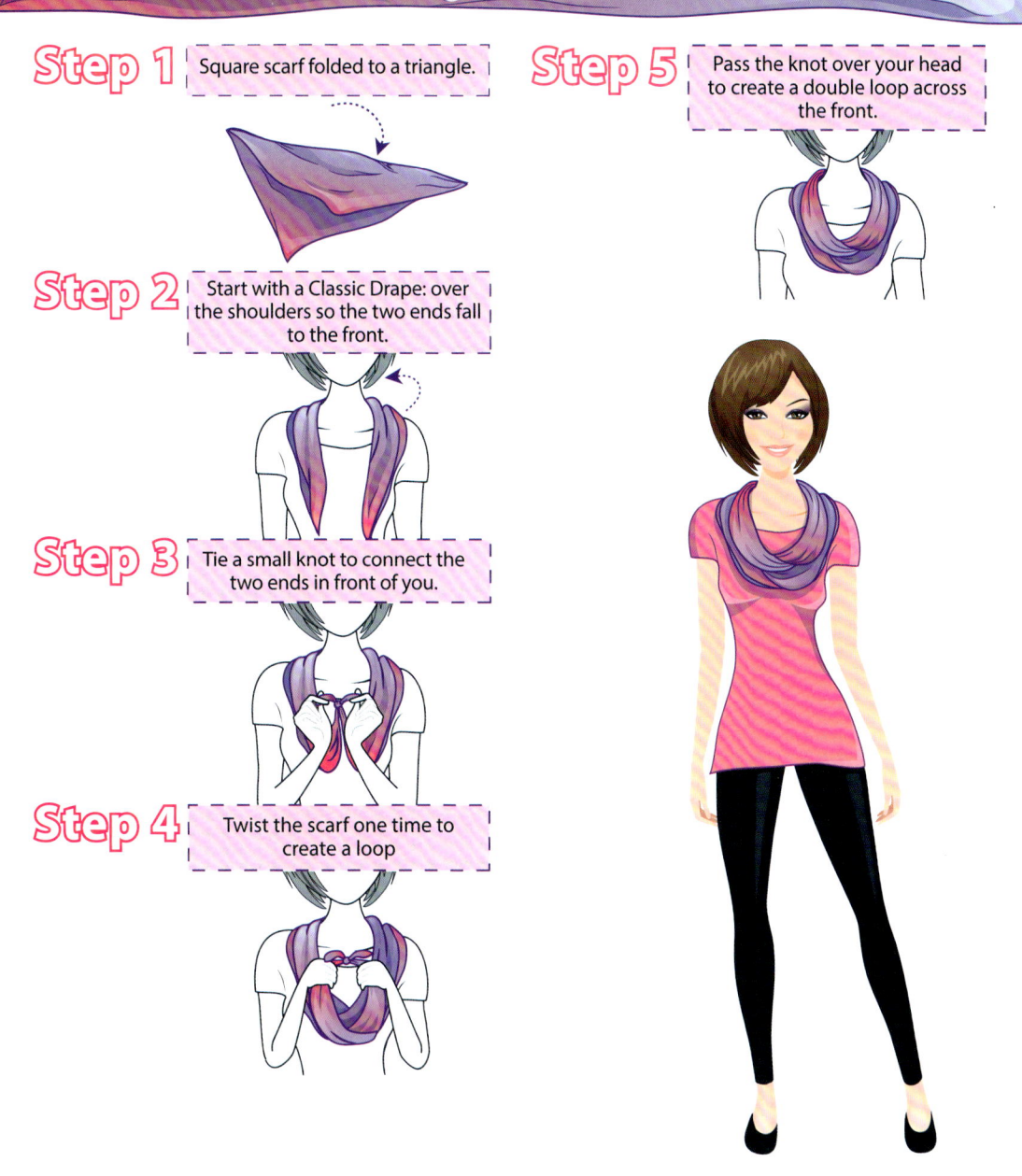

Step 1 — Square scarf folded to a triangle.

Step 2 — Start with a Classic Drape: over the shoulders so the two ends fall to the front.

Step 3 — Tie a small knot to connect the two ends in front of you.

Step 4 — Twist the scarf one time to create a loop

Step 5 — Pass the knot over your head to create a double loop across the front.

This is a terrific and simple way to turn any large lightweight square scarf into a blousy accent for a simple dress or skirt and T-shirt summer look. It's also a great way to convert any of your favorite scarves into an infinity loop without having to buy a whole new wardrobe of infinity scarves.
Turn your favorite scarf into an infinity scarf with one simple knot!

Knot 14: The Waterfall

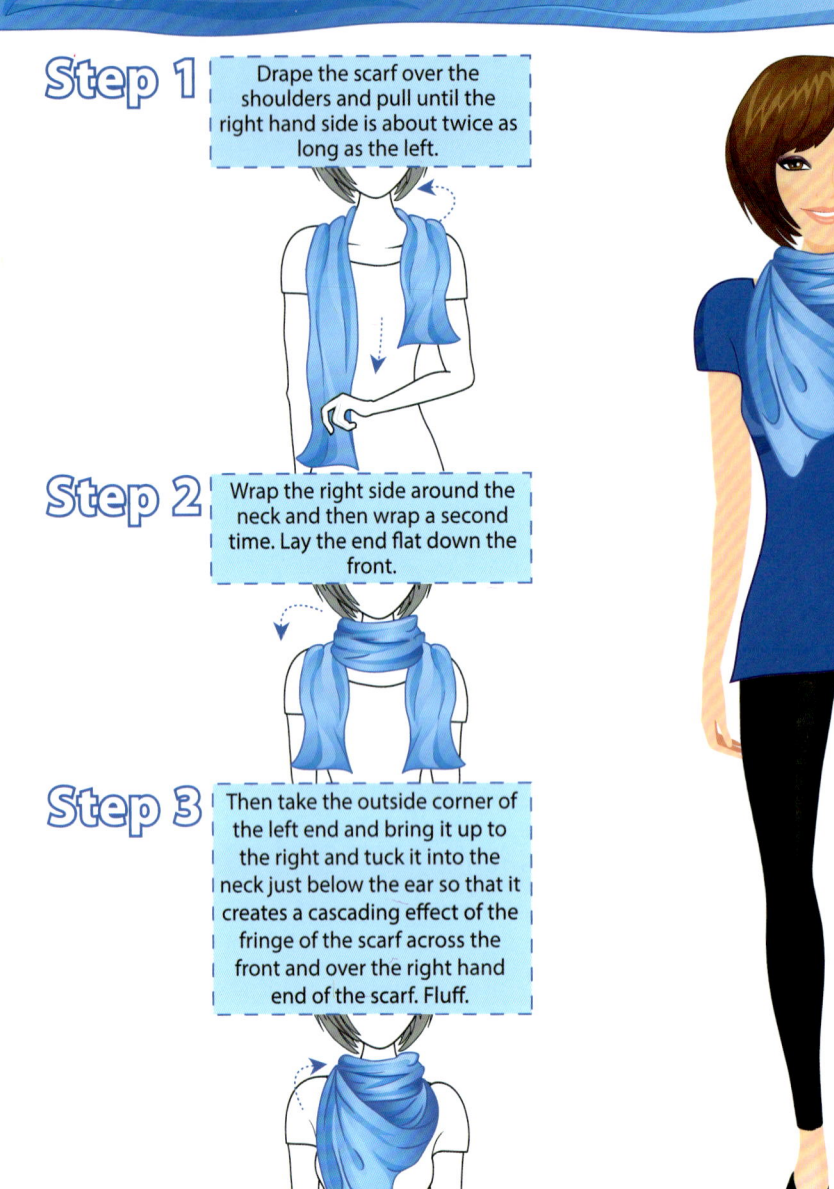

Step 1 — Drape the scarf over the shoulders and pull until the right hand side is about twice as long as the left.

Step 2 — Wrap the right side around the neck and then wrap a second time. Lay the end flat down the front.

Step 3 — Then take the outside corner of the left end and bring it up to the right and tuck it into the neck just below the ear so that it creates a cascading effect of the fringe of the scarf across the front and over the right hand end of the scarf. Fluff.

This knot uses a long rectangular scarf. This is a really classy look for cool weather – and works wonderfully with a large full cashmere rectangle scarf. The cashmere is soft and light enough to fall gracefully and the fringe is delicate and pretty.

For a dramatic effect use a solid rich color and contrast it with large shiny dangle earrings.

Knot 15: The Simple Bolero

Step 1 — Drape the scarf over the shoulders to the front so that both ends hang evenly.

Step 2 — Bring the ends back under the arms to the center of the back and tie together.

Step 3 — Arrange the 'sleeves' over the shoulders and evenly across the upper arms.

A great way to wear a scarf to keep away the chill on a cool spring night, this is a stylish tie for a large scarf with a pattern. Just be sure the pattern is right side up when you drape the scarf over the shoulders.

Knot 16: The Decoration

Step 1 — Drape the scarf over the shoulders so the left side is slightly longer than the right side.

Step 2 — Tie a single loop knot in the left end at about the height of your collar bone by passing the scarf through itself in a single loop.

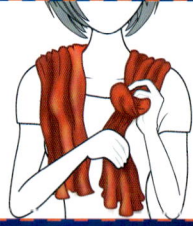

Step 3 — Place the decoration at the top of the knot with the stem or bobby pin hanging down inside the knot. Hold it in place keeping the knot loose.

Step 4 — Now pass the right hand end down through the loop and, holding the decoration, gently cinch the knot tighter and up closer to the chin so that the decoration sits on top of the loop knot and the two ends hang straight down below.

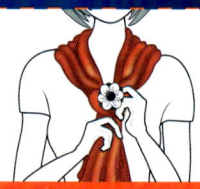

This knot uses a rectangle scarf and a decoration such as an artificial flower with a stem or a hair decoration attached to a bobby pin.

Knot 17: The Lady's Half Windsor

Step 1: Start with a square scarf folded on the diagonal as follows: Lay the scarf on a flat surface like a diamond with one point facing you. Fold the bottom point up to just past the midpoint of the scarf.

Step 2: Fold the top point down to just inside the bottom fold you just created.

Step 3: Now fold the bottom up to the center so it lines up with the scarf points on either side.

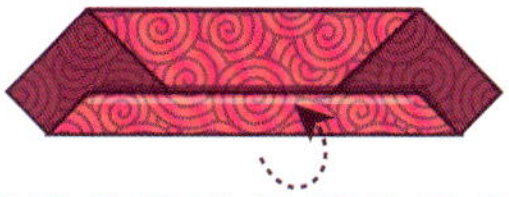

Step 4: Next, fold the top edge down to just above the bottom fold.

Step 5: Finally, fold the entire scarf in half lengthwise once more.

Step 6: Drape the scarf over the shoulders so the right hand side is longer than the left.

Step 7: Hold the left end in place with your left hand. Wrap the right end across the front of the left and behind the back to the right.

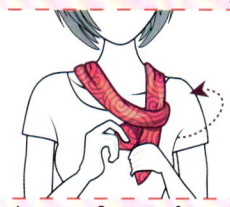

Step 8: Now place two fingers of your left hand across the forming knot and wrap the right end across those two fingers to the left.

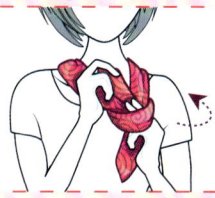

Step 9: This time, instead of coming back out to the right, come up through the loop around your neck. Now thread the right end down into the loop held open by your fingers and pull down from below to tighten.

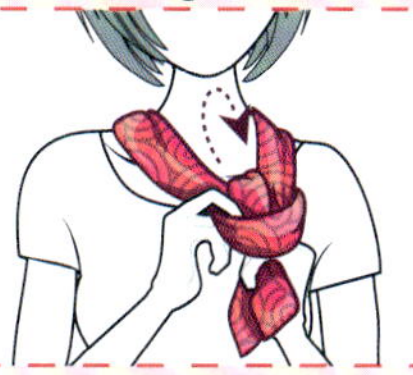

Step 10: Adjust the loose ends.

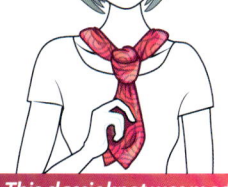

This classic knot was made famous by Annie Hall and is a neck tie knot everyone should know. Folding a square designer scarf on the diagonal will give it a very classy look.

19

Knot 18: Ascot

Step 1 — Start with a square scarf folded on the diagonal as follows: Lay the scarf on a flat surface like a diamond with one point facing you. Fold the bottom point up to just past the midpoint of the scarf.

Step 2 — Fold the top point down to just inside the bottom fold you just created.

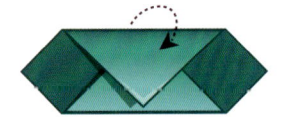

Step 3 — Now fold the bottom up to the center so it lines up with the scarf points on either side.

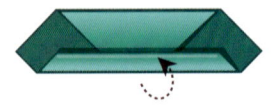

Step 4 — Next, fold the top edge down to just above the bottom fold.

Step 5 — Finally, fold the entire scarf in half lengthwise once more.

Step 6 — Drape the scarf around the neck so ends hang down the front evenly on each side.

Step 7 — Take the right end and bring it over the left end and tie a simple knot by bringing the left end up, over and around the right end. The right end is now on the left and becomes the top of the knot.

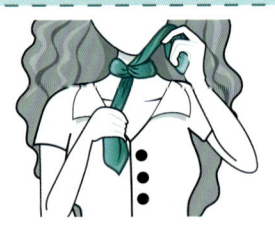

Step 8 — Hold the two ends in the left hand using your fingers to keep them separate creating a space between them.

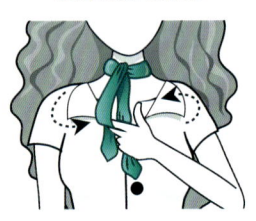

Quick, easy and highly versatile this knot works just about anywhere with lots of different fashions.

Knot 18: Ascot

Step 9

Using your right hand draw the top (right hand) end above your left hand and behind both ends and to the left

Step 10

Continue to hold both ends in place with your left hand. Push your right hand between the two ends above the left hand. Grab the right end which is hanging over the left hand, and draw it back through the space between the two ends to tie the second knot. Cinch neatly.

Step 11

Wrap the scarf ends behind the neck and make a small knot. Tuck the ends underneath.

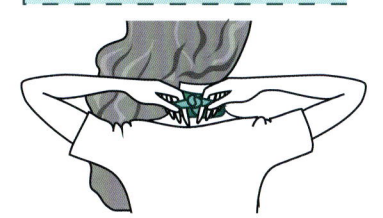

21

Knot 19: Buckaroo or Four Square Knot

Step 1 — Drape the scarf over your shoulders so the two ends hang down the front with the left side longer than the right.

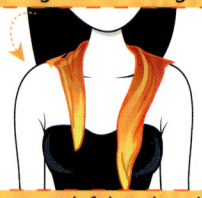

Step 2 — Place your left hand under the left end and wrap the end around the middle and index fingers of your left hand.

Step 3 — Pass the right end under the left end and in front of the left hand.

Step 4 — Now circle back around to the right, behind both sides of the scarf.

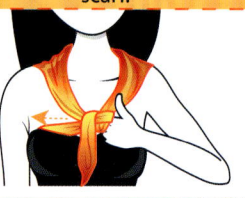

Step 5 — Pass the right end over the left end and then under the loop you've just formed.

Step 6 — Tighten up the knot so that all four squares are even.

This is a traditional knot that was well known and used in the Old West in the U.S. by cowboys wearing 'wild rags', also called cowboy bandanas and neckerchiefs. These are large square silk scarves, 36"-44" square is the traditional large size. Interesting as this compares favorably to a Hermès Square, a famous designer scarf introduced by Hermès which was started by Thierry Hermès in 1837 as a fine handcrafted harness and bridle shop serving the carriage trade in Paris. They went on to develop a line of saddlery, and fine leather bags for their customers to use to carry their saddles when traveling overseas. In 1937 they introduced the Hermès Carré or Hermès Square as it is sometimes called in English. This knot uses a square scarf folded in half to a triangle. You can also pleat/fold the ends in layers for a neater look.

Knot 20: The Kelly Wrap

Step 1 — Fold the scarf in a triangle.

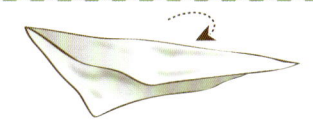

Step 2 — Bring the triangle over your head so the center of the long side is at the center of the top of your face and the two ends are hanging evenly down the sides in the front.

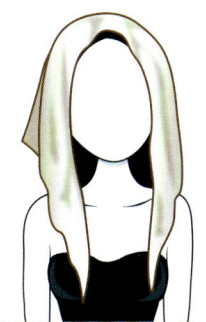

Step 3 — Bring the two ends across each other at the front of the neck but do not tie them.

Step 4 — Draw the two ends to the back of the neck and tie them in a loose knot to hold them in place.

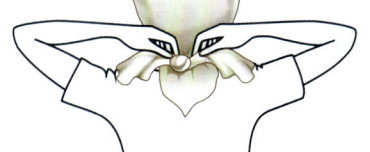

This classic scarf style was made famous by Grace Kelly, hence its name. Top it off with a pair of big sunglasses and you can go completely 'incognito'.
This tie works with a large square scarf or a medium sized oblong scarf.

23